# 40 Days
# of
# Power-Filled Prayer

*Spiritual Ammunition for Victorious Kingdom Living*

## Jamelle E. McKenzie

Published by:

Salt and Light Media
3588 Highway 138 Suite 302
Stockbridge, GA 30281


info@saltandlightmedia.net

www.powerfilledprayer.org


ISBN: 978-0-9884281-0-2 (*sc*)

*Printed in the United States of America*


*Unless otherwise indicated, all scripture quotations are taken from the King James Version of the Bible*

# FOREWARD

The purpose of this manual is to provide the reader with spiritual ammunition to launch a lifestyle of power filled prayer. One of the last things Jesus requested of His disciples before His crucifixion was that they spend time in prayer with Him. It is my sincere belief that even now Jesus is beckoning to His Bride, His church to spend time in prayer. Unfortunately we have become so overwhelmed with the trivia of day to day life that we fail to make this call to prayer a priority. Then we ask ourselves why our ministries are weak, failing and ineffective and our spiritual lives lack fervency. I invite you to take the next forty days to plunge into the Word of God and prayer. Now get started…..Kingdom life is awaiting.

This book is dedicated to the beautiful people of Destiny Tabernacle International and Adullam Ministries nightly Prayer Line who continue to prevail in love and righteousness through power filled prayer.

The Journey Begins.............

The Journey Continues.............

# Getting Started

God gave me specific plans before having me write this manual on how He wanted me to lead believers in the Body of Christ to fulfill their Kingdom mandate. The exercises in this booklet are spiritually and scientifically designed to strengthen your Kingdom walk and to move you into a life filled with the Glory and manifestation of God. It is important that you follow each exercise and be diligent.

Identify an accountability partner who will be your prayer mate during this time and meet with them each day to spend time in prayer. This guide will give you scripture and direction for your journey. The chapters are broken down into seven weeks designed for you to start on a Wednesday and end on a Sunday. I purposefully neglected to include written prayers as so many devotional books of this nature do because the words for your prayers must come directly from you to God, and that's what makes your prayers so powerful, because they will be from your heart to the heart of God.

During this 40 Day period find opportunities to emerge yourself in prayer as much as possible independently and with others. Attend prayer meeting and arrive in time for intercessory prayer at your local assembly. Join a prayer group or call into a prayer line. The Adullam Ministries' prayer line* is available every evening at 7:00pm EST if you would like to participate.

Now prepare yourself for a journey designed to transform your entire life – 40 Days of Power-Filled Prayer!

*Adullam Ministries' prayer line meets every night at 7pm EST. Dial (712)432-3900 Access code 6949061

# Week 1 – I am Delivered

You are an eternal spirit that possesses a transformable soul and lives in an earthly body. When God created you, your spirit was made in His likeness and in His image. This means that you were made by God to be just like God. Now you are not God but you are like Him. The trespass of Adam resulted in the fall of all mankind bringing each of us to a state where we became separated from God as well as our understanding of who and what God created us to be. In order to redeem us, or bring us back to our former state, God did something awesome and out of this world. He took a part of Himself in the person of Christ Jesus and had Jesus take on an earthly form to demonstrate to us how to live on earth, and then offer His body for us, so that we could be restored to our heavenly likeness and image. God who originally made us like His Own Self lowered Himself from His Self to become like the ones He created in order to get us to once again be like His Self. This is marvelous!!! Through Jesus God has not only redeemed and restored us spirit, soul and body but has also given us the pattern or the "How to" be like Him while still occupying these earthly bodies. If you have received Jesus as your Lord and Savior then you have not only been restored to eternal life, but also eternal living starting the moment you accepted Him into your heart. This is the beginning of deliverance. Deliverance is an event, a state and a process. God brought the event through Jesus and your acceptance of Jesus led you to the state of being delivered. Now the process of reconciling your life to the Life of Jesus continues daily. You are delivered to be delivered, remain delivered, and live delivered so you can deliver!

*Romans 5*
*King James Version (KJV)*

*5 Therefore being justified by faith, we have peace with God through our Lord Jesus Christ*

*:2 By whom also we have access by faith into this grace wherein we stand, and rejoice in hope of the glory of God.*

*3 And not only so, but we glory in tribulations also: knowing that tribulation worketh patience*

*;4 And patience, experience; and experience, hope:5 And hope maketh not ashamed; because the love of God is shed abroad in our hearts by the Holy Ghost which is given unto us.*

*6 For when we were yet without strength, in due time Christ died for the ungodly*

*.7 For scarcely for a righteous man will one die: yet peradventure for a good man some would even dare to die*

*.8 But God commendeth his love toward us, in that, while we were yet sinners, Christ died for us.*

*9 Much more then, being now justified by his blood, we shall be saved from wrath through him.*

*10 For if, when we were enemies, we were reconciled to God by the death of his Son, much more, being reconciled, we shall be saved by his life.*

*11 And not only so, but we also joy in God through our Lord Jesus Christ, by whom we have now received the atonement.*

*12 Wherefore, as by one man sin entered into the world, and death by sin; and so death passed upon all men, for that all have sinned:*

*13 (For until the law sin was in the world: but sin is not imputed when there is no law.*

*14 Nevertheless death reigned from Adam to Moses, even over them that had not sinned after the similitude of Adam's transgression, who is the figure of him that was to come.*

*15 But not as the offence, so also is the free gift. For if through the offence of one many be dead, much more the grace of God, and the gift by grace, which is by one man, Jesus Christ, hath abounded unto many.*

*16 And not as it was by one that sinned, so is the gift: for the judgment was by one to condemnation, but the free gift is of many offences unto justification.*

*17 For if by one man's offence death reigned by one; much more they which receive abundance of grace and of the gift of righteousness shall reign in life by one, Jesus Christ.)*

*18 Therefore as by the offence of one judgment came upon all men to condemnation; even so by the righteousness of one the free gift came upon all men unto justification of life.*

*19 For as by one man's disobedience many were made sinners, so by the obedience of one shall many be made righteous.*

*20 Moreover the law entered, that the offence might abound. But where sin abounded, grace did much more abound:*

*21 That as sin hath reigned unto death, even so might grace reign through righteousness unto eternal life by Jesus Christ our Lord.*

**Day One – Wednesday      Colossians 1:12-18**(KJV)

*12 Giving thanks unto the Father, which hath made us meet to be partakers of the inheritance of the saints in light:13 Who hath delivered us from the power of darkness, and hath translated us into the kingdom of his dear Son:14 In whom we have redemption through his blood, even the forgiveness of sins:15 Who is the image of the invisible God, the firstborn of every creature:*

*16 For by him were all things created, that are in heaven, and that are in earth, visible and invisible, whether they be thrones, or dominions, or principalities, or powers: all things were created by him, and for him:17 And he is before all things, and by him all things consist.18 And he is the head of the body, the church: who is the beginning, the firstborn from the dead; that in all things he might have the preeminence.*

**Daily Empowerment:**

Write three godly confessions about yourself and who you are based on the verses of Scripture above. Share them with your prayer partner. Confess your prayer partner's confessions for themselves as well.

1._____

2._____

3._____

Five things I am praying about today are:

1._____

2._____

3._____

4._____

5._____

Five People I am Praying For Today are:

1._____

2._____

3._____

4._____

5._____

**Day Two**     **Galatians 5:1, 7, 13-26** (KJV)

*5 Stand fast therefore in the liberty wherewith Christ hath made us free, and be not entangled again with the yoke of bondage.*

*7 Ye did run well; who did hinder you that ye should not obey the truth?*

*13 For, brethren, ye have been called unto liberty; only use not liberty for an occasion to the flesh, but by love serve one another. 14 For all the law is fulfilled in one word, even in this; Thou shalt love thy neighbour as thyself. 15 But if ye bite and devour one another, take heed that ye be not consumed one of another.*

*16 This I say then, Walk in the Spirit, and ye shall not fulfil the lust of the flesh. 17 For the flesh lusteth against the Spirit, and the Spirit against the flesh: and these are contrary the one to the other: so that ye cannot do the things that ye would. 18 But if ye be led of the Spirit, ye are not under the law.*

*19 Now the works of the flesh are manifest, which are these; Adultery, fornication, uncleanness, lasciviousness, 20 Idolatry, witchcraft, hatred, variance, emulations, wrath, strife, seditions, heresies, 21 Envyings, murders, drunkenness, revellings, and such like: of the which I tell you before, as I have also told you in time past, that they which do such things shall not inherit the kingdom of God.*

*22 But the fruit of the Spirit is love, joy, peace, longsuffering, gentleness, goodness, faith, 23 Meekness, temperance: against such there is no law. 24 And they that are Christ's have crucified the flesh with the affections and lusts. 25 If we live in the Spirit, let us also walk in the Spirit. 26 Let us not be desirous of vain glory, provoking one another, envying one another.*

### Daily Empowerment:

What are three areas where you could take a better stand? Write them down in the form of a positive confession. For example, if you are struggling with envy because of jealousy towards what others have, your confession will be "I am happy to see others blessed and I thank God for giving me every blessing that is just for me". Share them with your prayer partner. Confess your prayer partner's confessions for themselves as well.

My standing confessions are:

1._____

2._____

3._____

Five things I am praying about today are:

1._____

2._____

3._____

4._____

5._____

Five People I am Praying For Today are:

1._____

2._____

3._____

4._____

5._____

**Day Three**                    **Daniel 3:14-30** (KJV)

*14 Nebuchadnezzar spake and said unto them, Is it true, O Shadrach, Meshach, and Abednego, do not ye serve my gods, nor worship the golden image which I have set up? 15 Now if ye be ready that at what time ye hear the sound of the cornet, flute, harp, sackbut, psaltery, and dulcimer, and all kinds of musick, ye fall down and worship the image which I have made; well: but if ye worship not, ye shall be cast the same hour into the midst of a burning fiery furnace; and who is that God that shall deliver you out of my hands?*

*16 Shadrach, Meshach, and Abednego, answered and said to the king, O Nebuchadnezzar, we are not careful to answer thee in this matter. 17 If it be so, our God whom we serve is able to deliver us from the burning fiery furnace, and he will deliver us out of thine hand, O king. 18 But if not, be it known unto thee, O king, that we will not serve thy gods, nor worship the golden image which thou hast set up.*

*19 Then was Nebuchadnezzar full of fury, and the form of his visage was changed against Shadrach, Meshach, and Abednego: therefore he spake, and commanded that they should heat the furnace one seven times more than it was wont to be heated. 20 And he commanded the most mighty men that were in his army to bind Shadrach, Meshach, and Abednego, and to cast them into the burning fiery furnace. 21 Then these men were bound in their coats, their hosen, and their hats, and their other garments, and were cast into the midst of the burning fiery furnace. 22 Therefore because the king's commandment was urgent, and the furnace exceeding hot, the flames of the fire slew those men that took up Shadrach, Meshach, and Abednego.*

*23 And these three men, Shadrach, Meshach, and Abednego, fell down bound into the midst of the burning fiery furnace. 24 Then Nebuchadnezzar the king was astonished, and rose up in haste, and spake, and said unto his counsellors, Did not we cast three men bound into the midst of the fire? They answered and said unto the king, True, O king. 25 He answered and said, Lo, I see four men loose, walking in the midst of the fire, and they have no hurt; and the form of the fourth is like the Son of God.*

*26 Then Nebuchadnezzar came near to the mouth of the burning fiery furnace, and spake, and said, Shadrach, Meshach, and Abednego, ye servants of the most high God, come forth, and come hither. Then Shadrach, Meshach, and Abednego, came forth of the midst of the fire. 27 And the princes, governors, and captains, and the king's counsellors, being gathered together, saw these men, upon whose bodies the fire had no power, nor was an hair of their head singed, neither were their coats changed, nor the smell of fire had passed on them.*

*28 Then Nebuchadnezzar spake, and said, Blessed be the God of Shadrach, Meshach, and Abednego, who hath sent his angel, and delivered his servants that trusted in him, and have changed the king's word, and yielded their bodies, that they might not serve nor worship any god, except their own God. 29 Therefore I make a decree, That every people, nation, and language, which speak any thing amiss against the God of Shadrach, Meshach, and Abednego, shall be cut in pieces, and their houses shall be made a dunghill: because there is no other God that can deliver after this sort.*

**30** *Then the king promoted Shadrach, Meshach, and Abednego, in the province of Babylon.*

## Daily Empowerment:

There is no circumstance too hard for God. The very thing that seems so difficult for us is easy for Him. What was it about these young Hebrew boys that caused them to refuse to bow down to man in the face of adversity, but rather to stand tall? It was their faith and trust in God as God and as their One True, Only Deliverer. Whatever circumstances you may be facing past, present and future you must believe that God is "Able". Refuse to give in, or to give up when you know that God has you where He wants you. If you are not in place, hurry up and get there and stand! Write three areas that you would like to encourage your prayer partner to stand and share them with your prayer partner today:

I am encouraging my prayer partner in the following areas:

1._____

2._____

3._____

Five things I am praying about today are:

1._____

2._____

3._____

4._____

5._____

Five People I am Praying For Today are:

1._____

2._____

3._____

4._____

5._____

**Day Four**  **Psalm 91**(KJV)

**91** *He that dwelleth in the secret place of the most High shall abide under the shadow of the Almighty.* [2] *I will say of the* LORD, *He is my refuge and my fortress: my God; in him will I trust.* [3] *Surely he shall deliver thee from the snare of the fowler, and from the noisome pestilence.*

[4] *He shall cover thee with his feathers, and under his wings shalt thou trust: his truth shall be thy shield and buckler.* [5] *Thou shalt not be afraid for the terror by night; nor for the arrow that flieth by day;* [6] *Nor for the pestilence that walketh in darkness; nor for the destruction that wasteth at noonday.*

[7] *A thousand shall fall at thy side, and ten thousand at thy right hand; but it shall not come nigh thee.* [8] *Only with thine eyes shalt thou behold and see the reward of the wicked.* [9] *Because thou hast made the* LORD, *which is my refuge, even the most High, thy habitation;*

[10] *There shall no evil befall thee, neither shall any plague come nigh thy dwelling.* [11] *For he shall give his angels charge over thee, to keep thee in all thy ways.* [12] *They shall bear thee up in their hands, lest thou dash thy foot against a stone.*

[13] *Thou shalt tread upon the lion and adder: the young lion and the dragon shalt thou trample under feet.* [14] *Because he hath set his love upon me, therefore will I deliver him: I will set him on high, because he hath known my name.* [15] *He shall call upon me, and I will answer him: I will be with him in trouble; I will deliver him, and honour him.*

[16] *With long life will I satisfy him, and shew him my salvation.*

## Daily Empowerment:

One of the many beautiful things about God's deliverance in our life is the fact that whenever He delivers us "out from" something He always delivers us "in to" something better. He doesn't bring us out just to leave us hanging. We are delivered from trouble to dwell in His safety net. Once we decide to stay in His fortress where we are safe, we will remain safe as we keep our trust in Him. When we trust God and remain hidden in Him we become immune to the effects of the troubles that may surround us. Where is your trust today? Are you hidden? Discuss the following confession with your prayer partner today after writing down three situations where you have seen God's protection and immunity at work in your life.

**_"My refuge in God has made me immune to every circumstance around me that does not resemble heaven."_**

1._____

2._____

3._____

Five things I am praying about today are:

1._____

2._____

3._____

4._____

5._____


Five People I am Praying For Today are:

1._____

2._____

3._____

4._____

5._____

# Week 2 – I am Consecrated

Once we come into the realization that we are made in the image and likeness of God (Genesis 1:26-27), it becomes apparent that we cannot continue to live on earth as a body that has a spirit but rather as a spirit that has a body. When this mental transition begins to occur inside of us we find ourselves in even greater need of a relationship with God, The Father, like never before. This is the catalyst that causes us to begin to live from our true eternal heavenly place rather than from earth's temporal physical deception. Furthermore, the knowledge that our bodies are truly the temple of the living God catapults us into a lifestyle of pleasing the Master rather than gratifying the passions of this physical fleshy house. You no longer want to sin anymore, not just because sin is wrong, but now sin becomes a disgrace, a stain, a disappointment to the God that lives within. The desire for holiness and righteousness becomes first and foremost and we find ourselves in that state of wanting to be here to fulfill the purpose of God for our lives rather than just for a new house or car. Consecration to God is the vehicle that opens our hearts to reach this most blessed state of being and it is the fuel that keeps us in the proper frame of mind needed for God to have His way in our lives and for the Kingdom of God to flow through us and manifest from us. Consecration is the release of what's in your hand and opening yourself to what is in the Hands of God for you and for those around you.

**John 17:1-23**
*King James Version (KJV)*

**17** *These words spake Jesus, and lifted up his eyes to heaven, and said, Father, the hour is come; glorify thy Son, that thy Son also may glorify thee:* **2** *As thou hast given him power over all flesh, that he should give eternal life to as many as thou hast given him.* **3** *And this is life eternal, that they might know thee the only true God, and Jesus Christ, whom thou hast sent.* **4** *I have glorified thee on the earth: I have finished the work which thou gavest me to do.* **5** *And now, O Father, glorify thou me with thine own self with the glory which I had with thee before the world was.* **6** *I have manifested thy name unto the men which thou gavest me out of the world: thine they were, and thou gavest them me; and they have kept thy word.* **7** *Now they have known that all things whatsoever thou hast given me are of thee.*

**8** *For I have given unto them the words which thou gavest me; and they have received them, and have known surely that I came out from thee, and they have believed that thou didst send me.* **9** *I pray for them: I pray not for the world, but for them which thou hast given me; for they are thine.* **10** *And all mine are thine, and thine are mine; and I am glorified in them.* **11** *And now I am no more in the world, but these are in the world, and I come to thee. Holy Father, keep through thine own name those whom thou hast given me, that they may be one, as we are.*

*12 While I was with them in the world, I kept them in thy name: those that thou gavest me I have kept, and none of them is lost, but the son of perdition; that the scripture might be fulfilled. 13 And now come I to thee; and these things I speak in the world, that they might have my joy fulfilled in themselves. 14 I have given them thy word; and the world hath hated them, because they are not of the world, even as I am not of the world. 15 I pray not that thou shouldest take them out of the world, but that thou shouldest keep them from the evil.*

*16 They are not of the world, even as I am not of the world. 17 Sanctify them through thy truth: thy word is truth. 18 As thou hast sent me into the world, even so have I also sent them into the world. 19 And for their sakes I sanctify myself, that they also might be sanctified through the truth.*

*20 Neither pray I for these alone, but for them also which shall believe on me through their word; 21 That they all may be one; as thou, Father, art in me, and I in thee, that they also may be one in us: that the world may believe that thou hast sent me. 22 And the glory which thou gavest me I have given them; that they may be one, even as we are one: 23 I in them, and thou in me, that they may be made perfect in one; and that the world may know that thou hast sent me, and hast loved them, as thou hast loved me.*

**Day Five**          **Romans 12:1-2** (KJV)

*12 I beseech you therefore, brethren, by the mercies of God, that ye present your bodies a living sacrifice, holy, acceptable unto God, which is your reasonable service.² And be not conformed to this world: but be ye transformed by the renewing of your mind, that ye may prove what is that good, and acceptable, and perfect, will of God.*

**Daily Empowerment:**

What does it mean to be transformed? Look up the definition, write it below and discuss with your prayer partner the process of transformation in your life.

Definition of Transform:

_____

I am transforming by doing the following:

1._____

2._____

Five things I am praying about today are:

1._____

2._____

3._____

4._____

5._____

Five People I am Praying For Today are:

1._____

2._____

3._____

4._____

5._____

**Day Six**                    **Ephesians 1:3,4** (KJV)

*3 Blessed be the God and Father of our Lord Jesus Christ, who hath blessed us with all spiritual blessings in heavenly places in Christ:4 According as he hath chosen us in him before the foundation of the world, that we should be holy and without blame before him in love:*

**Ephesians 2:5-7**(KJV)

*5 Even when we were dead in sins, hath quickened us together with Christ, (by grace ye are saved;)6 And hath raised us up together, and made us sit together in heavenly places in Christ Jesus:7 That in the ages to come he might shew the exceeding riches of his grace in his kindness toward us through Christ Jesus.*

**Daily Empowerment:**

These two scriptures from Ephesians make it evident that not only are we seated in heavenly places in Christ but our blessings are also located in those same heavenly places. This is why it is detrimental to our Kingdom walk to for us to live from our heavenly place in Christ Jesus, rather than to place our focus on what our eyes see on earth. Create three Kingdom of God minded confessions to share with your prayer partner today that will help them keep their focus in their heavenly place.

Three Heavenly Confessions for my prayer partner:

1._____

2._____

3._____

Five things I am praying about today are:

1._____

2._____

3._____

4._____

5._____

Five People I am Praying For Today are:

1._____

2._____

3._____

4._____

5._____

**Day Seven**                    **Colossians 3:1-11**(KJV)

**3** *If ye then be risen with Christ, seek those things which are above, where Christ sitteth on the right hand of God.*² *Set your affection on things above, not on things on the earth.*³ *For ye are dead, and your life is hid with Christ in God.*⁴ *When Christ, who is our life, shall appear, then shall ye also appear with him in glory.*

⁵ *Mortify therefore your members which are upon the earth; fornication, uncleanness, inordinate affection, evil concupiscence, and covetousness, which is idolatry:*⁶ *For which things' sake the wrath of God cometh on the children of disobedience:*⁷ *In the which ye also walked some time, when ye lived in them.*

⁸ *But now ye also put off all these; anger, wrath, malice, blasphemy, filthy communication out of your mouth.*⁹ *Lie not one to another, seeing that ye have put off the old man with his deeds;*¹⁰ *And have put on the new man, which is renewed in knowledge after the image of him that created him:*¹¹ *Where there is neither Greek nor Jew, circumcision nor uncircumcision, Barbarian, Scythian, bond nor free: but Christ is all, and in all.*

## Daily Empowerment:

List three things to seek after that are from above. Share them with your prayer partner.

Three Heavenly things we need to seek after are:

1._____

2._____

3._____

Five things I am praying about today are:

1._____

2._____

3._____

4._____

5._____

Five People I am Praying For Today are:

1._____

2._____

3._____

4._____

5._____

**Day Eight**          **Philippians 4:8-9** (KJV)

*⁸ Finally, brethren, whatsoever things are true, whatsoever things are honest, whatsoever things are just, whatsoever things are pure, whatsoever things are lovely, whatsoever things are of good report; if there be any virtue, and if there be any praise, think on these things.⁹ Those things, which ye have both learned, and received, and heard, and seen in me, do: and the God of peace shall be with you.*

**Daily Empowerment:**

We are able to keep our affections set on things that are above by continuing to think on what is listed in the verses above. If we find ourselves encumbered with thoughts that do not line up with this list, it's time to make an immediate change. Share with your prayer partner an incident in your life when you changed your thinking from "stinking thinking" to one of the thoughts listed above. Discuss the outcome.

An incident when I changed my "stinking thinking" to "godly thinking was:

_____

_____

Five things I am praying about today are:

1._____

2._____

3._____

4._____

5._____

Five People I am Praying For Today are:

1._____

2._____

3._____

4._____

5._____

**Day Nine**                    **1 Peter 1:13-16**(KJV)

*13 Wherefore gird up the loins of your mind, be sober, and hope to the end for the grace that is to be brought unto you at the revelation of Jesus Christ;14 As obedient children, not fashioning yourselves according to the former lusts in your ignorance:*

*15 But as he which hath called you is holy, so be ye holy in all manner of conversation;16 Because it is written, Be ye holy; for I am holy.*

**Daily Empowerment:**

What does it mean to be holy? Write your own definition and share it with your prayer partner. Discuss why you believe holiness is important to God and a requirement for His people.

To Be Holy Is:

_____

_____

Five things I am praying about today are:

1._____

2._____

3._____

4._____

5._____

Five People I am Praying For Today are:

1._____

2._____

3._____

4._____

5._____

**Day Ten**                    **Joshua 1:7-9** (KJV)

*⁷ Only be thou strong and very courageous, that thou mayest observe to do according to all the law, which Moses my servant commanded thee: turn not from it to the right hand or to the left, that thou mayest prosper withersoever thou goest.*

*⁸ This book of the law shall not depart out of thy mouth; but thou shalt meditate therein day and night, that thou mayest observe to do according to all that is written therein: for then thou shalt make thy way prosperous, and then thou shalt have good success. ⁹ Have not I commanded thee? Be strong and of a good courage; be not afraid, neither be thou dismayed: for the LORD thy God is with thee whithersoever thou goest.*

**Daily Empowerment:**

One of the main components of consecration is meditating on the word of God. As we meditate on God's Word our mind is filled with His thoughts and His ways thus making it easier for us to live in His Will because our way of thinking changes. Find three verses of scripture in the bible to give your prayer partner to incorporate into their personal meditation.

Three Scriptures for My Prayer Partner's Meditation are:

1._____

2._____

3._____

Five things I am praying about today are:

1._____

2._____

3._____

4._____

5._____

Five People I am Praying For Today are:

1._____

2._____

3._____

4._____

5._____

**Day Eleven**                    **1 Chronicles 16:11**(KJV)

*[11] Seek the LORD and his strength, seek his face continually.*

**Daily Empowerment:**

This verse from 1 Chronicles may not be wordy, but the few words it contains speak volumes. In order to truly consecrate ones' life to God our focus must be about God. Our heart must be after His heart. We must recognize that any and all strength we have comes from Him. Set goals or a plan for how you can seek God's face continually. Share the information with your prayer partner.

I plan to seek God continually by:

1._____

2._____

3._____

Five things I am praying about today are:

1._____

2._____

3._____

4._____

5._____

Five People I am Praying For Today are:

1._____

2._____

3._____

4._____

5._____

# Week Three – I am a Worshipper

One of the most misunderstood components of the Christian lifestyle is "worship". Often when believers are asked why they worship God their answers are vague and shallow or filled with church jargon because in all actuality we take worshipping God for granted and really have not given much thought to it. Many believers are so ignorant of the importance of worship that they purposefully plan to arrive at church just in time to hear the message so that they don't have to stand for twenty or so minutes while the praise team "sings". Worship goes way beyond the praise team's selections for Sunday morning or the worship leader's pleas to get us to clap or raise our hands.

Worship is both a verb and a noun. According to *Webster's Dictionary*, its verb form includes such synonyms as "esteem," "exalt," "revere," "glorify" and "respect." As a noun, it can encompass adoration, devotion, supplication and invocation. Its actual definition, though, is "reverence, honor or homage paid to God; ceremonies or services expressing such reverence." Worship includes both an attitude and the actions that accompany and are motivated by it.

*The Dictionary of Biblical Imagery* says, "Worship is first and foremost a verb, an action" (p.970). This is revealing because so many equate worship with either a place (usually a building) or a feeling. That worship is an action becomes clearer when we examine the roots of the Hebrew and Greek words for "worship." According to the *New Bible Dictionary*, both the "Hebrew *aboda*, and the Greek*latreia* originally signified the labor of slaves or hired servants" (p. 1262). Therefore, the underlying concept of worship in Scripture is that of service to the One revered. This understanding greatly expands the application of worship far beyond the walls of a building. It includes any activity done in service to and because of the one worshipped.*

Worship is a lifestyle of expression of our respect, adoration and reverence to God, our Creator. It must be woven into the fabric of everything we do. As we submit our daily activities to God, acknowledging Him in all we do, giving Him praise and thanksgiving for who He is and what He has done, our every action becomes representative of who He is and thus we glorify Him on earth as He is glorified in heaven.

*http://www.cgg.org/index.cfm/fuseaction/Library.sr/CT/personal/k/64/Why-Worship-God.htm

## Psalm 66

King James Version (KJV)

**66** *Make a joyful noise unto God, all ye lands:*

*² Sing forth the honour of his name: make his praise glorious.³ Say unto God, How terrible art thou in thy works! through the greatness of thy power shall thine enemies submit themselves unto thee.*

*⁴ All the earth shall worship thee, and shall sing unto thee; they shall sing to thy name. Selah.⁵ Come and see the works of God: he is terrible in his doing toward the children of men.⁶ He turned the sea into dry land: they went through the flood on foot: there did we rejoice in him.⁷ He ruleth by his power for ever; his eyes behold the nations: let not the rebellious exalt themselves. Selah.*

*⁸ O bless our God, ye people, and make the voice of his praise to be heard:⁹ Which holdeth our soul in life, and suffereth not our feet to be moved.¹⁰ For thou, O God, hast proved us: thou hast tried us, as silver is tried.¹¹ Thou broughtest us into the net; thou laidst affliction upon our loins.¹² Thou hast caused men to ride over our heads; we went through fire and through water: but thou broughtest us out into a wealthy place.*

*¹³ I will go into thy house with burnt offerings: I will pay thee my vows,¹⁴ Which my lips have uttered, and my mouth hath spoken, when I was in trouble.¹⁵ I will offer unto thee burnt sacrifices of fatlings, with the incense of rams; I will offer bullocks with goats. Selah.*

*¹⁶ Come and hear, all ye that fear God, and I will declare what he hath done for my soul.¹⁷ I cried unto him with my mouth, and he was extolled with my tongue.¹⁸ If I regard iniquity in my heart, the Lord will not hear me:¹⁹ But verily God hath heard me; he hath attended to the voice of my prayer.²⁰ Blessed be God, which hath not turned away my prayer, nor his mercy from me.*

**Day Twelve**                    **Psalm 37:3-7** (KJV)

*³ Trust in the LORD, and do good; so shalt thou dwell in the land, and verily thou shalt be fed.*

*⁴ Delight thyself also in the LORD: and he shall give thee the desires of thine heart.*

*⁵ Commit thy way unto the LORD; trust also in him; and he shall bring it to pass.*

*⁶ And he shall bring forth thy righteousness as the light, and thy judgment as the noonday.⁷ Rest in the LORD, and wait patiently for him: fret not thyself because of him who prospereth in his way, because of the man who bringeth wicked devices to pass.*

## Daily Empowerment:

As we trust in the Lord and delight ourselves in Him, committing our ways to Him, we are worshipping Him by demonstrating to Him that He truly is our God. The term "delight" actually means to "find pleasure" in the Lord. When we find our happiness and pleasure in God not only is He able to release things that we desire to us but He is also able to shape our desires! Wouldn't it be wonderful to want only what God wants. This way we would never be let down because He would only give us the desires for things He was planning to do for us in the first place. What are some desires that you need to turn over to God? Share up to three with your prayer partner.

I am submitting the following desires to God:

1._____

2._____

3._____

Five things I am praying about today are:

1._____

2._____

3._____

4._____

5._____

Five People I am Praying For Today are:

1._____

2._____

3._____

4._____

5._____

**Day Thirteen**　　　　　**John 4:23-24** (KJV)

*23 But the hour cometh, and now is, when the true worshippers shall worship the Father in spirit and in truth: for the Father seeketh such to worship him.*

*24 God is a Spirit: and they that worship him must worship him in spirit and in truth.*

**Daily Empowerment:**

What does it mean to worship God in spirit and in truth? Have a discussion with your prayer partner about how to worship the Father in spirit and in truth. Write your notes from this discussion below:

Notes from our "spirit and truth" discussion:

_____

_____

_____

Five things I am praying about today are:

1._____

2._____

3._____

4._____

5._____

Five People I am Praying For Today are:

1._____

2._____

3._____

4._____

5._____

**Day Fourteen**　　　　**1 Thessalonians 5:16-24** (KJV)

*16 Rejoice evermore.*

*17 Pray without ceasing.*

*18 In every thing give thanks: for this is the will of God in Christ Jesus concerning you.*

*19 Quench not the Spirit.*

*20 Despise not prophesyings.*

*21 Prove all things; hold fast that which is good.*

*22 Abstain from all appearance of evil.*

*23 And the very God of peace sanctify you wholly; and I pray God your whole spirit and soul and body be preserved blameless unto the coming of our Lord Jesus Christ. 24 Faithful is he that calleth you, who also will do it.*

**Daily Empowerment:**

Which items listed above in verses 16-22 could be considered worship? Write them down and share and compare with your prayer partner.

Worship is:

_____

_____

_____

Five things I am praying about today are:

1._____

2._____

3._____

4._____

5._____

Five People I am Praying For Today are:

1._____

2._____

3._____

4._____

5._____

**Day Fifteen**          **Psalm 34:1-9** (KJV)

*34 I will bless the LORD at all times: his praise shall continually be in my mouth.² My soul shall make her boast in the LORD: the humble shall hear thereof, and be glad.³ O magnify the LORD with me, and let us exalt his name together.*

*⁴ I sought the LORD, and he heard me, and delivered me from all my fears.⁵ They looked unto him, and were lightened: and their faces were not ashamed.⁶ This poor man cried, and the LORD heard him, and saved him out of all his troubles.*

*⁷ The angel of the LORD encampeth round about them that fear him, and delivereth them.⁸ O taste and see that the LORD is good: blessed is the man that trusteth in him.⁹ O fear the LORD, ye his saints: for there is no want to them that fear him.*

**Daily Empowerment:**

When is the right time to praise and worship God? At all times!!!! David gives his testimony of worship in the Psalm above. What is your worship testimony? Write it below and share it with your prayer partner.

My Praise and Worship Testimony:

_____

Five things I am praying about today are:

1._____

2._____

3._____

4._____

5._____

Five People I am Praying For Today are:

1._____

2._____

3._____

4._____

5._____

**Day Sixteen**                    **Exodus 20:2-17** (KJV)

*² I am the LORD thy God, which have brought thee out of the land of Egypt, out of the house of bondage.*

*³ Thou shalt have no other gods before me.*

*⁴ Thou shalt not make unto thee any graven image, or any likeness of any thing that is in heaven above, or that is in the earth beneath, or that is in the water under the earth.*

*⁵ Thou shalt not bow down thyself to them, nor serve them: for I the LORD thy God am a jealous God, visiting the iniquity of the fathers upon the children unto the third and fourth generation of them that hate me;*

*⁶ And shewing mercy unto thousands of them that love me, and keep my commandments.*

*⁷ Thou shalt not take the name of the LORD thy God in vain; for the LORD will not hold him guiltless that taketh his name in vain.*

*⁸ Remember the sabbath day, to keep it holy.*

*⁹ Six days shalt thou labour, and do all thy work:*

*¹⁰ But the seventh day is the sabbath of the LORD thy God: in it thou shalt not do any work, thou, nor thy son, nor thy daughter, thy manservant, nor thy maidservant, nor thy cattle, nor thy stranger that is within thy gates:*

*¹¹ For in six days the LORD made heaven and earth, the sea, and all that in them is, and rested the seventh day: wherefore the LORD blessed the sabbath day, and hallowed it.*

*¹² Honour thy father and thy mother: that thy days may be long upon the land which the LORD thy God giveth thee.*

*¹³ Thou shalt not kill.*

*¹⁴ Thou shalt not commit adultery.*

*¹⁵ Thou shalt not steal.*

*¹⁶ Thou shalt not bear false witness against thy neighbour.*

*¹⁷ Thou shalt not covet thy neighbour's house, thou shalt not covet thy neighbour's wife, nor his manservant, nor his maidservant, nor his ox, nor his ass, nor any thing that is thy neighbour's.*

Daily Empowerment:

The children of Israel were given the ten commandments by God through Moses to show them how to properly worship God. How do these commandments apply to you today? Discuss this with your prayer partner and record the notes from your discussion below:

How the Ten Commandments Apply to My Life today:

_____

_____

_____

Five things I am praying about today are:

1._____

2._____

3._____

4._____

5._____

Five People I am Praying For Today are:

1._____

2._____

3._____

4._____

5._____

**Day Seventeen**    Joshua 6:1-27(KJV)

**6** *Now Jericho was straitly shut up because of the children of Israel: none went out, and none came in.* **2** *And the LORD said unto Joshua, See, I have given into thine hand Jericho, and the king thereof, and the mighty men of valour.* **3** *And ye shall compass the city, all ye men of war, and go round about the city once. Thus shalt thou do six days.* **4** *And seven priests shall bear before the ark seven trumpets of rams' horns: and the seventh day ye shall compass the city seven times, and the priests shall blow with the trumpets* **5** *And it shall come to pass, that when they make a long blast with the ram's horn, and when ye hear the sound of the trumpet, all the people shall shout with a great shout; and the wall of the city shall fall down flat, and the people shall ascend up every man straight before him.* **6** *And Joshua the son of Nun called the priests, and said unto them, Take up the ark of the covenant, and let seven priests bear seven trumpets of rams' horns before the ark of the LORD.* **7** *And he said unto the people, Pass on, and compass the city, and let him that is armed pass on before the ark of the LORD.*

**8** *And it came to pass, when Joshua had spoken unto the people, that the seven priests bearing the seven trumpets of rams' horns passed on before the LORD, and blew with the trumpets: and the ark of the covenant of the LORD followed them.* **9** *And the armed men went before the priests that blew with the trumpets, and the rereward came after the ark, the priests going on, and blowing with the trumpets.* **10** *And Joshua had commanded the people, saying, Ye shall not shout, nor make any noise with your voice, neither shall any word proceed out of your mouth, until the day I bid you shout; then shall ye shout.* **11** *So the ark of the LORD compassed the city, going about it once: and they came into the camp, and lodged in the camp.*

**12** *And Joshua rose early in the morning, and the priests took up the ark of the LORD.* **13** *And seven priests bearing seven trumpets of rams' horns before the ark of the LORD went on continually, and blew with the trumpets: and the armed men went before them; but the rereward came after the ark of theLORD, the priests going on, and blowing with the trumpets.* **14** *And the second day they compassed the city once, and returned into the camp: so they did six days.* **15** *And it came to pass on the seventh day, that they rose early about the dawning of the day, and compassed the city after the same manner seven times: only on that day they compassed the city seven times.* **16** *And it came to pass at the seventh time, when the priests blew with the trumpets, Joshua said unto the people, Shout; for the LORD hath given you the city.* **17** *And the city shall be accursed, even it, and all that are therein, to the LORD: only Rahab the harlot shall live, she and all that are with her in the house, because she hid the messengers that we sent.* **18** *And ye, in any wise keep yourselves from the accursed thing, lest ye make yourselves accursed, when ye take of the accursed thing, and make the camp of Israel a curse, and trouble it.* **19** *But all the silver, and gold, and vessels of brass and iron, are consecrated unto the LORD: they shall come into the treasury of the LORD.*

**20** *So the people shouted when the priests blew with the trumpets: and it came to pass, when the people heard the sound of the trumpet, and the people shouted* *with a great shout, that the wall fell down flat, so that the people went up into the city, every man straight before him, and they took the city.* [21] *And they utterly destroyed all that was in the city, both man and woman, young and old, and ox, and sheep, and ass, with the edge of the sword.*

Daily Empowerment:

The story of the battle of Jericho demonstrates the effectiveness of praise and worship. The Israelites had need of no weapon but praise in their defeat of Jericho. What battles are you losing that could be won simply by submitting yourself to God through praise and worship? Share ways to incorporate worship into life battles with your prayer partner.

I can incorporate worship into the following situations for victory:

1._____

2._____

3._____

Five things I am praying about today are:

1._____

2._____

3._____

4._____

5._____

Five People I am Praying For Today are:

1._____

2._____

3._____

4._____

5._____

**Day Eighteen**       **1 Chronicles 16:28-30** (KJV)

*28 Give unto the LORD, ye kindreds of the people, give unto the LORD glory and strength.29 Give unto the LORD the glory due unto his name: bring an offering, and come before him: worship the LORD in the beauty of holiness.30 Fear before him, all the earth: the world also shall be stable, that it be not moved.*

Daily Empowerment:

This scripture gives us insight to an aspect of worship that we often take lightly and tend to neglect – giving. Yes giving an offering is an extension of your worship. Furthermore, our worship brings stability to the conditions of the world around us. Discuss with your prayer partner how you can "step up" your worship.

I plan to "step up" my worship in the following ways:

1._____

2._____

3._____

Five things I am praying about today are:

1._____

2._____

3._____

4._____

5._____

Five People I am Praying For Today are:

1._____

2._____

3._____

4._____

5._____

# Week Four – I Love

As a young Christian I was mistakenly led to think that people who had powerful ministry gifts operating in their lives, with signs and wonders and/or large crowds or congregations following them, were somewhat closer to God than the rest of us. I wanted Him to bless me with signs, wonders, spiritual gifts and numbers to show me He was close to me and me to Him. After a few years of seeking God's greatness, He revealed to me the avenue for what really counts with Him and to Him – Love. He began to expose me to several large ministries and well known celebrity preachers, and allowed me to see that several of them were missing this main ingredient - Love for Him, Love for themselves and Love for the people around them. I made up my mind at that moment that I would aim for greatness in my love walk. God showed me that wherever He was present there would be an uncompromising atmosphere of genuine love. He has helped me to see throughout my years of ministry that at the end of the day all that really counts is love – because that's what He is. When we try to operate in ministry outside of the Love of God, we may get results but they may not be orchestrated or manifested by the Spirit of the Lord. When we love God, an intimate relationship forms in which we who are already known by God get to actually know God for ourselves. It is the Father's desire that we be one with Him, because after all that's where we originated and He wants us to remain connected to our home. If you are looking for anything other than the love of God, stop right now and redirect yourself to the heart of God. It is a total win-win situation. As you grow deeper in love with the Lord, He ushers you into His awesome presence where not only do you love Him but you also begin to love yourself from a godly perspective. This love then allows you to love others and everyone in your life in a manner that your natural emotions are not even capable of. Live a life of love.

### 1 Corinthians 13
*New International Version (NIV)*

**13** *If I speak in the tongues[a] of men or of angels, but do not have love, I am only a resounding gong or a clanging cymbal. ² If I have the gift of prophecy and can fathom all mysteries and all knowledge, and if I have a faith that can move mountains, but do not have love, I am nothing. ³ If I give all I possess to the poor and give over my body to hardship that I may boast,[b] but do not have love, I gain nothing.*

*4 Love is patient, love is kind. It does not envy, it does not boast, it is not proud. 5 It does not dishonor others, it is not self-seeking, it is not easily angered, it keeps no record of wrongs. 6 Love does not delight in evil but rejoices with the truth. 7 It always protects, always trusts, always hopes, always perseveres.*

*8 Love never fails. But where there are prophecies, they will cease; where there are tongues, they will be stilled; where there is knowledge, it will pass away. 9 For we know in part and we prophesy in part, 10 but when completeness comes, what is in part disappears. 11 When I was a child, I talked like a child, I thought like a child, I reasoned like a child. When I became a man, I put the ways of childhood behind me. 12 For now we see only a reflection as in a mirror; then we shall see face to face. Now I know in part; then I shall know fully, even as I am fully known.*

*13 And now these three remain: faith, hope and love. But the greatest of these is love.*

**Day Nineteen**                    **Matthew 22:35-40** (KJV)

*[35] Then one of them, which was a lawyer, asked him a question, tempting him, and saying,[36] Master, which is the great commandment in the law?*

*[37] Jesus said unto him, Thou shalt love the Lord thy God with all thy heart, and with all thy soul, and with all thy mind.[38] This is the first and great commandment.[39] And the second is like unto it, Thou shalt love thy neighbour as thyself.[40] On these two commandments hang all the law and the prophets.*

## Daily Empowerment:

Several days ago we examined the Ten Commandments to determine whether they are still applicable in our lives today. Interesting enough Jesus tells us in these verses above that if we love God with everything in us and then our neighbors we can fulfill all of His commandments without trying to keep a record of each one. Share your definition of love with your prayer partner.

Love is:

_____

Five things I am praying about today are:

1._____

2._____

3._____

4._____

5._____

Five People I am Praying For Today are:

1._____

2._____

3._____

4._____

5._____

**Day Twenty**                    **Romans 13:8-11**(KJV)

*⁸ Owe no man anything, but to love one another: for he that loveth another hath fulfilled the law.⁹ For this, Thou shalt not commit adultery, Thou shalt not kill, Thou shalt not steal, Thou shalt not bear false witness, Thou shalt not covet; and if there be any other commandment, it is briefly comprehended in this saying, namely, Thou shalt love thy neighbour as thyself.¹⁰ Love worketh no ill to his neighbour: therefore love is the fulfilling of the law.¹¹ And that, knowing the time, that now it is high time to awake out of sleep: for now is our salvation nearer than when we believed.*

**Matthew 5:44-45**(KJV)

*⁴⁴ But I say unto you, Love your enemies, bless them that curse you, do good to them that hate you, and pray for them which despitefully use you, and persecute you;⁴⁵ That ye may be the children of your Father which is in heaven: for he maketh his sun to rise on the evil and on the good, and sendeth rain on the just and on the unjust.*

**Daily Empowerment:**

The first scripture gives the impression that love is a continual debt in our relationship with others. It also mentions that love causes us to treat others properly. Then the second scripture admonishes to love even our enemies. Share your thoughts on these verses with your prayer partner. Why is it so important to God for us to love others?

It is important to love others, even our enemies because:

_____

Five things I am praying about today are:

1._____

2._____

3._____

4._____

5._____

Five People I am Praying For Today are:

1._____

2._____

3._____

4._____

5._____

**Day Twenty-One**          **1 John 4:7-21**(KJV)

*7 Beloved, let us love one another: for love is of God; and every one that loveth is born of God, and knoweth God.*

*8 He that loveth not knoweth not God; for God is love.*

*9 In this was manifested the love of God toward us, because that God sent his only begotten Son into the world, that we might live through him.*

*10 Herein is love, not that we loved God, but that he loved us, and sent his Son to be the propitiation for our sins.*

*11 Beloved, if God so loved us, we ought also to love one another.*

*12 No man hath seen God at any time. If we love one another, God dwelleth in us, and his love is perfected in us.*

*13 Hereby know we that we dwell in him, and he in us, because he hath given us of his Spirit.*

*14 And we have seen and do testify that the Father sent the Son to be the Saviour of the world.*

*15 Whosoever shall confess that Jesus is the Son of God, God dwelleth in him, and he in God.*

*16 And we have known and believed the love that God hath to us. God is love; and he that dwelleth in love dwelleth in God, and God in him.*

*17 Herein is our love made perfect, that we may have boldness in the day of judgment: because as he is, so are we in this world.*

*18 There is no fear in love; but perfect love casteth out fear: because fear hath torment. He that feareth is not made perfect in love.*

*19 We love him, because he first loved us.*

*20 If a man say, I love God, and hateth his brother, he is a liar: for he that loveth not his brother whom he hath seen, how can he love God whom he hath not seen?*

*21 And this commandment have we from him, That he who loveth God love his brother also.*

**Daily Empowerment:**

These verses from 1 John 4 have make some very powerful statements about love. Select three verses to discuss with your prayer partner.

My three discussion verses from 1 John 4 are:

1._____

2._____

3._____

Five things I am praying about today are:

1._____

2._____

3._____

4._____

5._____

Five People I am Praying For Today are:

1._____

2._____

3._____

4._____

5._____

**Day Twenty-Two**                **John 15:11-17**(KJV)

*[11] These things have I spoken unto you, that my joy might remain in you, and that your joy might be full.[12] This is my commandment, That ye love one another, as I have loved you.*

*[13] Greater love hath no man than this, that a man lay down his life for his friends.[14] Ye are my friends, if ye do whatsoever I command you.[15] Henceforth I call you not servants; for the servant knoweth not what his lord doeth: but I have called you friends; for all things that I have heard of my Father I have made known unto you.*

*[16] Ye have not chosen me, but I have chosen you, and ordained you, that ye should go and bring forth fruit, and that your fruit should remain: that whatsoever ye shall ask of the Father in my name, he may give it you.[17] These things I command you, that ye love one another.*

### John 3:16-17(KJV)

*[16] For God so loved the world, that he gave his only begotten Son, that whosoever believeth in him should not perish, but have everlasting life.[17] For God sent not his Son into the world to condemn the world; but that the world through him might be saved.*

**Daily Empowerment:**

These scriptures demonstrate the side of love that sacrifices. What are some sacrifices you have made as a result of the Love of God operating within you? Share three of them with your prayer partner.

Three sacrifices I have made as a result of the Love of God operating in me are:

1._____

2._____

3._____

Five things I am praying about today are:

1._____

2._____

3._____

4._____

5._____

Five People I am Praying For Today are:

1._____

2._____

3._____

4._____

5._____

**Day Twenty-Three**          **Galatians 5:22-23**(KJV)

*²² But the fruit of the Spirit is love, joy, peace, longsuffering, gentleness, goodness, faith,²³ Meekness, temperance: against such there is no law.*

**Romans 5:5**(KJV)

*⁵ And hope maketh not ashamed; because the love of God is shed abroad in our hearts by the Holy Ghost which is given unto us.*

**Daily Empowerment:**

Love is a fruit of the Spirit of God given to us when we receive the Holy Ghost. There is nothing we need to do to get love than to receive God's Spirit. When God's spirit is present in a believer one of the main indicators is their ability to love. However because love is a fruit it will continue to grow in us which means we should always be excelling in our love. Make a list of three things you can do to grow in love. Share this list with your prayer partner.

Three things I am doing to grow in love are:

1._____

2._____

3._____

Five things I am praying about today are:

1._____

2._____

3._____

4._____

5._____

Five People I am Praying For Today are:

1._____

2._____

3._____

4._____

5._____

**Day Twenty-Four**         **1 Peter 4:7-9**(NIV)

*⁷ The end of all things is near. Therefore be alert and of sober mind so that you may pray. ⁸ Above all, love each other deeply, because love covers over a multitude of sins. ⁹ Offer hospitality to one another without grumbling.*

**Ephesians 5:1-2**(KJV)

*5 Be ye therefore followers of God, as dear children;² And walk in love, as Christ also hath loved us, and hath given himself for us an offering and a sacrifice to God for a sweet smelling savour.*

**Daily Empowerment:**

One critical component of love is forgiveness. When we walk in the love of God we are able to forgive others and overlook their short comings and imperfections because we realize that God has done the same for us. Recall a time in your life when you were faced with having to forgive someone or something by exercising the love of God. Share it with your prayer partner.

Walking in the love of God helped me forgive in the following situation:

_____

_____

Five things I am praying about today are:

1._____

2._____

3._____

4._____

5._____

Five People I am Praying For Today are:

1._____

2._____

3._____

4._____

5._____

**Day Twenty-Five**          **John 21:14-1** (KJV)

*14 This is now the third time that Jesus shewed himself to his disciples, after that he was risen from the dead. 15 So when they had dined, Jesus saith to Simon Peter, Simon, son of Jonas, lovest thou me more than these? He saith unto him, Yea, Lord; thou knowest that I love thee. He saith unto him, Feed my lambs.*

*16 He saith to him again the second time, Simon, son of Jonas, lovest thou me? He saith unto him, Yea, Lord; thou knowest that I love thee. He saith unto him, Feed my sheep. 17 He saith unto him the third time, Simon, son of Jonas, lovest thou me? Peter was grieved because he said unto him the third time, Lovest thou me? And he said unto him, Lord, thou knowest all things; thou knowest that I love thee. Jesus saith unto him, Feed my sheep.*

## Daily Empowerment:

A loving relationship with Jesus will always cause a child of God to be concerned about the needs of others. Why do you think Jesus had to tell Peter three times to feed His people? Is there something God has had to ask you to do more than once even though you answered "yes" the first time? Discuss your answers with your prayer partner.

Jesus had to tell Simon Peter to feed His people three times because:

_____

God has asked me to do the following more than once because:

_____

Five things I am praying about today are:

1._____

2._____

3._____

4._____

5._____

Five People I am Praying For Today are:

1._____

2._____

3._____

4._____

5._____

# Week Five – I am Powerful

Throughout the ages mankind has sought the possession of power. And in natural man's own twisted fashion humans have fabricated an illusion of power on the earth in order to control, oppress, enslave, dominate others and glorify their egos. However these forms of power and authority can in no fashion compare to or even come close to the power God has entrusted in each of His Blood washed, Spirit filled children. When the Father created each of us in His Own Image and His Own Likeness, He gave us the ability to possess the exact kind of power He has and the nature to go along with that power. Even though we experienced a setback in the Garden of Eden when Adam and Eve sinned, we were fully restored to our rightful place, position and authority when Jesus gave His Life on the Cross and then returned with all power which He invested back into us through the Holy Spirit. The issue with our power is that it doesn't come from earth but rather from heaven. Therefore we can't experience what God has given us by keeping our hearts, minds and eyes on what we see and experience in this three dimensional earthly realm. This is why The Father has given us seating in heavenly places in Christ Jesus. Our seating in heavenly places allows us to operate effectively on earth by being on one accord with God as we receive our direction directly from the Father. We then activate our power and authority by hearing and seeing what God said from heaven and agreeing with it by believing it and speaking it on earth. We are powerful.

## John 1:1-5, 10-13
King James Version (KJV)

*1 In the beginning was the Word, and the Word was with God, and the Word was God.² The same was in the beginning with God.³ All things were made by him; and without him was not anything made that was made.⁴ In him was life; and the life was the light of men.⁵ And the light shineth in darkness; and the darkness comprehended it not.*

*¹⁰ He was in the world, and the world was made by him, and the world knew him not.¹¹ He came unto his own, and his own received him not.*

*¹² But as many as received him, to them gave he power to become the sons of God, even to them that believe on his name:¹³ Which were born, not of blood, nor of the will of the flesh, nor of the will of man, but of God.*

**Day Twenty-Six**          **Acts 1:4-8**(KJV)

*⁴ And, being assembled together with them, commanded them that they should not depart from Jerusalem, but wait for the promise of the Father, which, saith he, ye have heard of me.*

*⁵ For John truly baptized with water; but ye shall be baptized with the Holy Ghost not many days hence.*

*⁶ When they therefore were come together, they asked of him, saying, Lord, wilt thou at this time restore again the kingdom to Israel?*

*⁷ And he said unto them, It is not for you to know the times or the seasons, which the Father hath put in his own power.*

*⁸ But ye shall receive power, after that the Holy Ghost is come upon you: and ye shall be witnesses unto me both in Jerusalem, and in all Judaea, and in Samaria, and unto the uttermost part of the earth.*

**Acts 2:1-4** (KJV)

*2 And when the day of Pentecost was fully come, they were all with one accord in one place.*

*² And suddenly there came a sound from heaven as of a rushing mighty wind, and it filled all the house where they were sitting.*

*³ And there appeared unto them cloven tongues like as of fire, and it sat upon each of them.*

*⁴ And they were all filled with the Holy Ghost, and began to speak with other tongues, as the Spirit gave them utterance.*

**Daily Empowerment:**

Power on earth is given to believers through the Holy Spirit. Ever since the day of Pentecost, God has made this power available. When we accept Christ as our personal savior the Holy Spirit makes his residence within us. But not only does God want His Sprit to reside in us, He wants us to be filled with His Spirit. Have you asked God to fill you (Baptize) with His Holy Spirit? Share your experience with your prayer partner. If you have not yet received the baptism of God's Holy Spirit this is the time to ask God.

My Baptism in the Holy Spirit: (Share your experience or pray with your prayer partner to be filled with the Holy Spirit)

_____

_____

Five things I am praying about today are:

1._____

2._____

3._____

4._____

5._____

Five People I am Praying For Today are:

1._____

2._____

3._____

4._____

5._____

## Day Twenty-Seven     1 Corinthians 1:18-25(KJV)

*<sup>18</sup> For the preaching of the cross is to them that perish foolishness; but unto us which are saved it is the power of God.*

*<sup>19</sup> For it is written, I will destroy the wisdom of the wise, and will bring to nothing the understanding of the prudent.<sup>20</sup> Where is the wise? where is the scribe? where is the disputer of this world? hath not God made foolish the wisdom of this world?*

*<sup>21</sup> For after that in the wisdom of God the world by wisdom knew not God, it pleased God by the foolishness of preaching to save them that believe.<sup>22</sup> For the Jews require a sign, and the Greeks seek after wisdom:*

*<sup>23</sup> But we preach Christ crucified, unto the Jews a stumblingblock, and unto the Greeks foolishness;<sup>24</sup> But unto them which are called, both Jews and Greeks, Christ the power of God, and the wisdom of God.<sup>25</sup> Because the foolishness of God is wiser than men; and the weakness of God is stronger than men.*

### Daily Empowerment:

This scripture refers to the "preaching of the cross" as being the power of God. The message of Jesus Christ within itself is powerful. You are empowered by sharing the message of Jesus to others and also by sharing your personal testimony of what Jesus has done for you. Share some of your personal testimony of what Christ has done in your life with your prayer partner.

My testimony in Christ Jesus:

_____

_____

Five things I am praying about today are:

1._____

2._____

3._____

4._____

5._____

Five People I am Praying For Today are:

1._____

2._____

3._____

4._____

5._____

## Day Twenty-Eight      1 Corinthians 12:3-11 (KJV)

*³ Wherefore I give you to understand, that no man speaking by the Spirit of God calleth Jesus accursed: and that no man can say that Jesus is the Lord, but by the Holy Ghost.*

*⁴ Now there are diversities of gifts, but the same Spirit.⁵ And there are differences of administrations, but the same Lord.⁶ And there are diversities of operations, but it is the same God which worketh all in all.*

*⁷ But the manifestation of the Spirit is given to every man to profit withal.⁸ For to one is given by the Spirit the word of wisdom; to another the word of knowledge by the same Spirit;⁹ To another faith by the same Spirit; to another the gifts of healing by the same Spirit;¹⁰ To another the working of miracles; to another prophecy; to another discerning of spirits; to another divers kinds of tongues; to another the interpretation of tongues:*

*¹¹ But all these worketh that one and the selfsame Spirit, dividing to every man severally as he will.*

### Daily Empowerment:

One of the ways God manifess His power through us is by giving us spiritual gifts. The verses above list nine spiritual gifts that have been given to allow us to be more effective in our lives and our service to others. What are your spiritual gifts? Discuss and share them with you prayer partner.

My Spiritual Gifts are:

_____

_____

Five things I am praying about today are:

1._____

2._____

3._____

4._____

5._____

Five People I am Praying For Today are:

1._____

2._____

3._____

4._____

5._____

## Day Twenty-Nine        Romans 12:3-13(KJV)

*³ For I say, through the grace given unto me, to every man that is among you, not to think of himself more highly than he ought to think; but to think soberly, according as God hath dealt to every man the measure of faith.⁴ For as we have many members in one body, and all members have not the same office:⁵ So we, being many, are one body in Christ, and every one members one of another.*

*⁶ Having then gifts differing according to the grace that is given to us, whether prophecy, let us prophesy according to the proportion of faith;⁷ Or ministry, let us wait on our ministering: or he that teacheth, on teaching;⁸ Or he that exhorteth, on exhortation: he that giveth, let him do it with simplicity; he that ruleth, with diligence; he that sheweth mercy, with cheerfulness.*

*⁹ Let love be without dissimulation. Abhor that which is evil; cleave to that which is good.¹⁰ Be kindly affectioned one to another with brotherly love; in honour preferring one another;¹¹ Not slothful in business; fervent in spirit; serving the Lord;¹² Rejoicing in hope; patient in tribulation; continuing instant in prayer;¹³ Distributing to the necessity of saints; given to hospitality.*

### Daily Empowerment:

Romans 12 gives another listing of spiritual gifts. This list includes more administrative gifts. These gifts are just as important as the nine gifts we looked at yesterday. Perhaps you did not see your gift on the 1 Corinthians 12 list or maybe you operate in a gift from this list as well. If your gift(s) is on the list above share and discuss it with your prayer partner. If not, pick one gift to discuss with your partner.

The gift I would like to discuss is:

_____

_____

Five things I am praying about today are:

1._____

2._____

3._____

4._____

5._____

Five People I am Praying For Today are:

1._____

2._____

3._____

4._____

5._____

**Day Thirty**                **Ephesians 4:8-16**(KJV)

*⁸ Wherefore he saith, When he ascended up on high, he led captivity captive, and gave gifts unto men.*

*⁹ (Now that he ascended, what is it but that he also descended first into the lower parts of the earth?*

*¹⁰ He that descended is the same also that ascended up far above all heavens, that he might fill all things.)*

*¹¹ And he gave some, apostles; and some, prophets; and some, evangelists; and some, pastors and teachers;*

*¹² For the perfecting of the saints, for the work of the ministry, for the edifying of the body of Christ:*

*¹³ Till we all come in the unity of the faith, and of the knowledge of the Son of God, unto a perfect man, unto the measure of the stature of the fulness of Christ:*

*¹⁴ That we henceforth be no more children, tossed to and fro, and carried about with every wind of doctrine, by the sleight of men, and cunning craftiness, whereby they lie in wait to deceive;*

*¹⁵ But speaking the truth in love, may grow up into him in all things, which is the head, even Christ:*

*¹⁶ From whom the whole body fitly joined together and compacted by that which every joint supplieth, according to the effectual working in the measure of every part, maketh increase of the body unto the edifying of itself in love.*

**Daily Empowerment:**

The gifts listed above are given to the church through the Holy Spirit in the form of people to empower the entire body of Christ. Select one of these five gifts from Ephesians and discuss with your prayer partner how that gift helps empower the Body of Christ. If you are one of these gifts discuss how God uses you to edify His Body.

The Ministry Gift I am discussing is:

_____

_____

Five things I am praying about today are:

1._____

2._____

3._____

4._____

5._____


Five People I am Praying For Today are:

1._____

2._____

3._____

4._____

5._____

**Day Thirty-One**          **Luke 11:5-10**(KJV)

*⁵ And he said unto them, Which of you shall have a friend, and shall go unto him at midnight, and say unto him, Friend, lend me three loaves;⁶ For a friend of mine in his journey is come to me, and I have nothing to set before him?*

*⁷ And he from within shall answer and say, Trouble me not: the door is now shut, and my children are with me in bed; I cannot rise and give thee.⁸ I say unto you, Though he will not rise and give him, because he is his friend, yet because of his importunity he will rise and give him as many as he needeth.*

*⁹ And I say unto you, Ask, and it shall be given you; seek, and ye shall find; knock, and it shall be opened unto you.¹⁰ For every one that asketh receiveth; and he that seeketh findeth; and to him that knocketh it shall be opened.*

## Daily Empowerment:

In order to walk in the power God has given to us we must participate by asking - verbalizing what we want or believe; seeking – having a heart after God that is willing to move beyond our comfort zone; and knocking – not being fearful, but rather assertive in our role as conquerors. Take one item from your list of five things to pray about today and discuss with your prayer partner how you plan to "seek" and "knock" once you have asked God.

My "seek" and "knock" plan for the following item I am praying about today is:

Item_____

My "seek" plan is:_____

My "knock" plan is:_____

Five things I am praying about today are:

1._____

2._____

3._____

4._____

5._____

Five People I am Praying For Today are:

1._____

2._____

3._____

4._____

5._____

**Day Thirty-Two**          **Matthew 16:18-19**(KJV)

*¹⁸ And I say also unto thee, That thou art Peter, and upon this rock I will build my church; and the gates of hell shall not prevail against it.*

*¹⁹ And I will give unto thee the keys of the kingdom of heaven: and whatsoever thou shalt bind on earth shall be bound in heaven: and whatsoever thou shalt loose on earth shall be loosed in heaven.*

Daily Empowerment:

One of the greatest pieces of knowledge every child of God needs to grab hold of is the fact that God has given us the power and the responsibility to determine what happens here on planet earth. If things aren't getting better down here and beginning to look more like heaven, it's our fault. We have been given the keys of the Kingdom of Heaven not to just walk around, jingling them in our pocket to occasionally pull out and threaten satan with them. We have the ability to put him out of business and lock out, lock up and shut down anything that's happening on earth that's not allowed in heaven. Furthermore, we have the ability to bring every good and perfect thing that resides in heaven to earth. What are some areas in your life, neighborhood, state, and country where you are just jingling the very keys that can change that situation? Share at least three with your prayer partner to day and begin to attack them immediately!

I will use my keys of the Kingdom to bring Heaven to the following:

1._____

2._____

3._____

Five things I am praying about today are:

1._____

2._____

3._____

4._____

5._____

Five People I am Praying For Today are:

1._____

2._____

3._____

4._____

5._____

# Week Six – I am Committed

Being committed is a state of dedicating oneself to a person, event, situation or thing. In the Old Testament the act of commitment was expressed in the form of covenants wherein believers pledged themselves to God and one another through vows, great sacrifices and even their own blood. One of the most important components of making a commitment is being willing to see something through past the ups and the downs the good in the bad, and the trials and the tests. This involves a sincere heart and a made up mind. Also when we commit ourselves we must be willing to give all of ourselves to the cause. We can't sit back and give 20%, then give up or complain because things didn't go the way we planned. We've got to involve 100% of ourselves if we are truly committed. Commitment affects and involves our entire being.

We must be committed to God and the purpose He has planned for our lives. Commitment requires faith and trust. We must have faith to see the end result regardless of how things appear from day to day. We must trust God throughout the process, from beginning to end and for eternity knowing that He holds us right in the palm of His Hands and will not let go. Adversity and familiarity are often the two greatest enemies of commitment. Adversity can cause hindrance because when times get tough we are often tempted to run. On the other hand familiarity can cause us to think we know everything ourselves or get us to become so comfortable that we begin to slack up and eventually slack off. Commitment can be summed up in the story of the tortoise and the hare. The hare was in a hurry and cocky because he knew he had more speed than the tortoise. Both of them were headed in the same direction, trying to reach the same goal, however only the tortoise was committed to getting to the finish line. It took him a long time but he won. He refused to give up or to give in. He did not allow himself to be distracted. This is what it means to be committed.

## Matthew 24:9-13
King James Version (KJV)

*⁹ Then shall they deliver you up to be afflicted, and shall kill you: and ye shall be hated of all nations for my name's sake.¹⁰ And then shall many be offended, and shall betray one another, and shall hate one another.¹¹ And many false prophets shall rise, and shall deceive many.¹² And because iniquity shall abound, the love of many shall wax cold.¹³ But he that shall endure unto the end, the same shall be saved.*

**Day Thirty-Three**          **Proverbs 16:1-3**(KJV)

**16** *The preparations of the heart in man, and the answer of the tongue, is from the LORD.² All the ways of a man are clean in his own eyes; but the LORD weigheth the spirits.³ Commit thy works unto the LORD, and thy thoughts shall be established.*

**Psalm 37:1-6**(KJV)

**37** *Fret not thyself because of evildoers, neither be thou envious against the workers of iniquity.² For they shall soon be cut down like the grass, and wither as the green herb.³ Trust in the LORD, and do good; so shalt thou dwell in the land, and verily thou shalt be fed.*

*⁴ Delight thyself also in the LORD: and he shall give thee the desires of thine heart.⁵ Commit thy way unto the LORD; trust also in him; and he shall bring it to pass.⁶ And he shall bring forth thy righteousness as the light, and thy judgment as the noonday.*

**Daily Empowerment:**

As we commit our works (what we do) and our ways (who we are, our character) to the Lord, God is able to manifest His Kingdom through us. You see God is not some genie who wants to give just anybody anything they want, He is concerned with every aspect of our being lining up with His so that we can truly live the God Kind of Life (Zoe) forever. When we are lined up with Him everything about us will bring the Glory back to Him from our thoughts to our desires and to our actions. What are some ways or works you need to commit totally to God. List up to three and share with your prayer partner.

I am committing my following works and/or ways to the Father:

1._____

2._____

3._____

Five things I am praying about today are:

1._____

2._____

3._____

4._____

5._____

Five People I am Praying For Today are:

1._____

2._____

3._____

4._____

5._____

## Day Thirty-Four  1 Corinthians 15:57-58(KJV)

*57 But thanks be to God, which giveth us the victory through our Lord Jesus Christ.58 Therefore, my beloved brethren, be ye stedfast, unmoveable, always abounding in the work of the Lord, forasmuch as ye know that your labour is not in vain in the Lord.*

### Philippians 3:13-15(KJV)

*13 Brethren, I count not myself to have apprehended: but this one thing I do, forgetting those things which are behind, and reaching forth unto those things which are before,14 I press toward the mark for the prize of the high calling of God in Christ Jesus15 Let us therefore, as many as be perfect, be thus minded: and if in anything ye be otherwise minded, God shall reveal even this unto you.*

### Daily Empowerment:

Commitment to God is a decision that leads to a process. It's going to take several ingredients in addition to a made up mind to remain committed. The two scriptures above list some of those ingredients. Identify at least three of these and share them with your prayer partner. Make sure to discuss why each ingredient you listed is important for one to have if they are to remain committed.

Three ingredients from the scriptures listed above that will help me to remain committed to God are:

1._____

2._____

3._____

Five things I am praying about today are:

1._____

2._____

3._____

4._____

5._____

Five People I am Praying For Today are:

1._____

2._____

3._____

4._____

5._____

**Day Thirty-Five**          **2 Corinthians 4:17-18**(KJV)

*17 For our light affliction, which is but for a moment, worketh for us a far more exceeding and eternal weight of glory;18 While we look not at the things which are seen, but at the things which are not seen: for the things which are seen are temporal; but the things which are not seen are eternal.*

**Hebrews 11:1-4**(KJV)

*11 Now faith is the substance of things hoped for, the evidence of things not seen.2 For by it the elders obtained a good report.3 Through faith we understand that the worlds were framed by the word of God, so that things which are seen were not made of things which do appear.*

**2 Corinthians 5:6-8**(KJV)

*6 Therefore we are always confident, knowing that, whilst we are at home in the body, we are absent from the Lord:7 (For we walk by faith, not by sight:)8 We are confident, I say, and willing rather to be absent from the body, and to be present with the Lord.*

**Daily Empowerment:**

Every committed believer must walk by faith in God. The moment we begin living by what our natural eyes and senses see and feel, our minds revert from our heavenly view clouding our ability to reign on earth through the power of the Kingdom of God. Write a letter to your prayer partner encouraging them to walk by faith based on the scriptures listed above. Share the letter with them when you meet today.

Encouraging Faith Letter to my prayer partner:

_____

_____

_____

_____

_____

_____

_____

Five things I am praying about today are:

1._____

2._____

3._____

4._____

5._____


Five People I am Praying For Today are:

1._____

2._____

3._____

4._____

5._____

## Day Thirty-Six     Hebrews 11:30 though Hebrews 12:3(KJV)

**30** *By faith the walls of Jericho fell down, after they were compassed about seven days.* **31** *By faith the harlot Rahab perished not with them that believed not, when she had received the spies with peace.* **32** *And what shall I more say? for the time would fail me to tell of Gedeon, and of Barak, and of Samson, and of Jephthae; of David also, and Samuel, and of the prophets:*

**33** *Who through faith subdued kingdoms, wrought righteousness, obtained promises, stopped the mouths of lions.* **34** *Quenched the violence of fire, escaped the edge of the sword, out of weakness were made strong, waxed valiant in fight, turned to flight the armies of the aliens.* **35** *Women received their dead raised to life again: and others were tortured, not accepting deliverance; that they might obtain a better resurrection:* **36** *And others had trial of cruel mockings and scourgings, yea, moreover of bonds and imprisonment:*

**37** *They were stoned, they were sawn asunder, were tempted, were slain with the sword: they wandered about in sheepskins and goatskins; being destitute, afflicted, tormented;* **38** *(Of whom the world was not worthy:) they wandered in deserts, and in mountains, and in dens and caves of the earth.* **39** *And these all, having obtained a good report through faith, received not the promise:* **40** *God having provided some better thing for us, that they without us should not be made perfect.*

**12** *Wherefore seeing we also are compassed about with so great a cloud of witnesses, let us lay aside every weight, and the sin which doth so easily beset us, and let us run with patience the race that is set before us,*

**2** *Looking unto Jesus the author and finisher of our faith; who for the joy that was set before him endured the cross, despising the shame, and is set down at the right hand of the throne of God.*

**3** *For consider him that endured such contradiction of sinners against himself, lest ye be wearied and faint in your minds.*

### Daily Empowerment:

These verses from chapters 11 and 12 of Hebrews give a sampling of some of the perils Old Testament believers went through as a result of their commitment to God. The verses end by expressing the joy Jesus experienced in order to keep His commitment concerning us, even though it involved sacrificing everything He had. The scripture implores us to lay aside anything that can get in the way of our keeping our commitment to Him. Take a moment to be honest and examine yourself. What things get in the way of your being totally committed to God? Write them down and pray about them with your prayer partner. Add them to your list of things to pray for in your personal prayer time as well.

Some things that hinder my being totally committed to God are:

1._____

2._____

3._____

Five things I am praying about today are:

1._____

2._____

3._____

4._____

5._____

Five People I am Praying For Today are:

1._____

2._____

3._____

4._____

5._____

**Day Thirty-Seven**          **Deuteronomy 28:1-14**(KJV)

*28 And it shall come to pass, if thou shalt hearken diligently unto the voice of the LORD thy God, to observe and to do all his commandments which I command thee this day, that the LORD thy God will set thee on high above all nations of the earth:² And all these blessings shall come on thee, and overtake thee, if thou shalt hearken unto the voice of the LORD thy God.*

*³ Blessed shalt thou be in the city, and blessed shalt thou be in the field.⁴ Blessed shall be the fruit of thy body, and the fruit of thy ground, and the fruit of thy cattle, the increase of thy kine, and the flocks of thy sheep.⁵ Blessed shall be thy basket and thy store.⁶ Blessed shalt thou be when thou comest in, and blessed shalt thou be when thou goest out.*

*⁷ The LORD shall cause thine enemies that rise up against thee to be smitten before thy face: they shall come out against thee one way, and flee before thee seven ways.⁸ The LORD shall command the blessing upon thee in thy storehouses, and in all that thou settest thine hand unto; and he shall bless thee in the land which the LORD thy God giveth thee.⁹ The LORD shall establish thee an holy people unto himself, as he hath sworn unto thee, if thou shalt keep the commandments of the LORD thy God, and walk in his ways.¹⁰ And all people of the earth shall see that thou art called by the name of the LORD; and they shall be afraid of thee.*

*¹¹ And the LORD shall make thee plenteous in goods, in the fruit of thy body, and in the fruit of thy cattle, and in the fruit of thy ground, in the land which the LORD sware unto thy fathers to give thee.¹² The LORD shall open unto thee his good treasure, the heaven to give the rain unto thy land in his season, and to bless all the work of thine hand: and thou shalt lend unto many nations, and thou shalt not borrow.*

*¹³ And the LORD shall make thee the head, and not the tail; and thou shalt be above only, and thou shalt not be beneath; if that thou hearken unto the commandments of the LORD thy God, which I command thee this day, to observe and to do them:¹⁴ And thou shalt not go aside from any of the words which I command thee this day, to the right hand, or to the left, to go after other gods to serve them.*

### Deuteronomy 8:6-18(KJV)

*⁶ Therefore thou shalt keep the commandments of the LORD thy God, to walk in his ways, and to fear him.⁷ For the LORD thy God bringeth thee into a good land, a land of brooks of water, of fountains and depths that spring out of valleys and hills;⁸ A land of wheat, and barley, and vines, and fig trees, and pomegranates; a land of oil olive, and honey;*

*⁹ A land wherein thou shalt eat bread without scarceness, thou shalt not lack any thing in it; a land whose stones are iron, and out of whose hills thou mayest dig* brass.**¹⁰** *When thou hast eaten and art full, then thou shalt bless the L*ORD *thy God for the good land which he hath given thee.*

**¹¹** *Beware that thou forget not the L*ORD *thy God, in not keeping his commandments, and his judgments, and his statutes, which I command thee this day:***¹²** *Lest when thou hast eaten and art full, and hast built goodly houses, and dwelt therein;***¹³** *And when thy herds and thy flocks multiply, and thy silver and thy gold is multiplied, and all that thou hast is multiplied;***¹⁴** *Then thine heart be lifted up, and thou forget the L*ORD *thy God, which brought thee forth out of the land of Egypt, from the house of bondage;***¹⁵** *Who led thee through that great and terrible wilderness, wherein were fiery serpents, and scorpions, and drought, where there was no water; who brought thee forth water out of the rock of flint;***¹⁶** *Who fed thee in the wilderness with manna, which thy fathers knew not, that he might humble thee, and that he might prove thee, to do thee good at thy latter end;***¹⁷** *And thou say in thine heart, My power and the might of mine hand hath gotten me this wealth.*

**¹⁸** *But thou shalt remember the L*ORD *thy God: for it is he that giveth thee power to get wealth, that he may establish his covenant which he sware unto thy fathers, as it is this day.*

## Daily Empowerment:

One of the many benefits of living an obedient life committed to God and His commands is the endless blessings that will roll out and overtake you. When we are committed to God we are in an attitude of constant remembrance, thankfulness and appreciation for all He has done for us and told us to do. Make a list of three blessings you have experienced over the past four weeks as a result of your commitment to praying daily with your prayer partner. Share them with your partner.

I have been blessed in the following ways as a result of my commitment to pray with my prayer partner:

1._____

2._____

3._____

Five things I am praying about today are:

1._____

2._____

3._____

4._____

5._____

Five People I am Praying For Today are:

1._____

2._____

3._____

4._____

5._____

**Day Thirty-Eight**          **Luke 18:1-9**(KJV)

*18 And he spake a parable unto them to this end, that men ought always to pray, and not to faint;*

*2 Saying, There was in a city a judge, which feared not God, neither regarded man:3 And there was a widow in that city; and she came unto him, saying, Avenge me of mine adversary.4 And he would not for a while: but afterward he said within himself, Though I fear not God, nor regard man;5 Yet because this widow troubleth me, I will avenge her, lest by her continual coming she weary me.*

*6 And the Lord said, Hear what the unjust judge saith.7 And shall not God avenge his own elect, which cry day and night unto him, though he bear long with them?8 I tell you that he will avenge them speedily. Nevertheless when the Son of man cometh, shall he find faith on the earth?9 And he spake this parable unto certain which trusted in themselves that they were righteous, and despised others:*

## Daily Empowerment:

In this scripture from Luke Jesus tells the story of a widow who was committed to getting a judge to give her legal protection against someone who was opposing her. Even though this judge didn't care anything about her or anyone else, he was compelled to help this lady because she was so consistent and would not give up. Now that you have been praying for 38 days, don't quit. Make a commitment to continue in prayer after this forty day experience. Begin now to plan your continued prayer life. Even if you were spending time in prayer before this time evaluate how you can "step your prayer life up" in the next few days. Share your plans with your prayer partner.

I will "step up" my prayer life at the end of these forty days by doing the following:

1._____

2._____

3._____

Five things I am praying about today are:

1._____

2._____

3._____

4._____

5._____

Five People I am Praying For Today are:

1._____

2._____

3._____

4._____

5._____

**Day Thirty-Nine**          **James 5:13-17**(KJV)

*¹³ Is any among you afflicted? let him pray. Is any merry? let him sing psalms.¹⁴ Is any sick among you? let him call for the elders of the church; and let them pray over him, anointing him with oil in the name of the Lord:¹⁵ And the prayer of faith shall save the sick, and the Lord shall raise him up; and if he have committed sins, they shall be forgiven him.*

*¹⁶ Confess your faults one to another, and pray one for another, that ye may be healed. The effectual fervent prayer of a righteous man availeth much.¹⁷ Elias was a man subject to like passions as we are, and he prayed earnestly that it might not rain: and it rained not on the earth by the space of three years and six months.*

**Daily Empowerment:**

As you continue in your commitment to God and to prayer it is essential that you don't find yourself sinking into a business as usual mentality of simply going through the motions to make sure your daily "T's" are crossed and "I's" are dotted. Effectualness and fervency are the key components to making your prayers and your life in the Kingdom of God power-filled! When you invoke effectualness into your prayers you are actually praying with results in mind. You are praying operative, effective prayers that bring about action and manifestation. When you are fervent you bring passion and intensity to your prayer life. This passion says to God and the angels that you are serious and every word you are saying has meaning and value and counts. Pray expecting God to move and pray until you yourself are moved. Have a discussion with your partner about how to remain effectual and fervent in prayer.

How to Stay Effectual and Fervent in my prayer life:

1._____

2._____

3._____

Five things I am praying about today are:

1._____

2._____

3._____

4._____

5._____

Five People I am Praying For Today are:

1._____

2._____

3._____

4._____

5._____

# Week Seven – I am a Servant

Jesus Christ is the greatest example of a true servant. Even though He was one with God, He left His position and humbled Himself to step into a human fleshly body made from dirt in a world that was ruled by the very beings he created. When He arrived here, he didn't live in 5 star hotels or a mansion with butlers and maids but rather His first day of human life was spent in a barn because there wasn't enough room in the bed and breakfast next to it for a man with a woman and a new born baby. He had all power yet he submitted Himself to natural parents, teachers, rabbis, rulers and government. After living on the planet for thirty years as a common citizen because He wasn't a part of the established political religious status quoi his ministry was devalued, criticized and ostracized. He was rejected by the very people He came to save, misunderstood by the ones He came to teach, and crucified by the very ones He gave the breath of life. Yet and still He completed what He came to do and He did it out of love and filled with joy. God from Heaven came to earth not to be served, but to serve and to give His life, a ransom for us all. As a servant He also gave us the greatest example of what true leadership is.

In order to be a God leader, one must remain a servant. Whether we admit it or acknowledge it, every child of God is leading in some capacity. The moment you open your mouth and tell someone you are a believer you become targeted as a leader. The unsaved world is constantly looking at children of God, how we act, the way we react, or our failure to act on a daily basis. We cannot win the lost to Christ without humbling ourselves as Jesus did. Separating and elevating ourselves on religious egotistical trips is not the answer. It doesn't help the unsaved nor does it assist the Body of Christ around us. Begin today entering the joy of serving others. Open your heart and mind to realize that every blessing bestowed on you is not just for you but it has been given so that you can better serve someone else. Remember you were created in the Image and Likeness of God. If we are truly representing Him we will also be doing just what He is and would be doing, the way He is and would be doing it. I have come to serve….

# John 15

King James Version (KJV)

**15** *I am the true vine, and my Father is the husbandman.*

*[2] Every branch in me that beareth not fruit he taketh away: and every branch that beareth fruit, he purgeth it, that it may bring forth more fruit.*

*[3] Now ye are clean through the word which I have spoken unto you.*

*[4] Abide in me, and I in you. As the branch cannot bear fruit of itself, except it abide in the vine; no more can ye, except ye abide in me.*

*[5] I am the vine, ye are the branches: He that abideth in me, and I in him, the same bringeth forth much fruit: for without me ye can do nothing.*

*[6] If a man abide not in me, he is cast forth as a branch, and is withered; and men gather them, and cast them into the fire, and they are burned.*

*[7] If ye abide in me, and my words abide in you, ye shall ask what ye will, and it shall be done unto you.*

*[8] Herein is my Father glorified, that ye bear much fruit; so shall ye be my disciples.*

*[9] As the Father hath loved me, so have I loved you: continue ye in my love.*

*[10] If ye keep my commandments, ye shall abide in my love; even as I have kept my Father's commandments, and abide in his love.*

*[11] These things have I spoken unto you, that my joy might remain in you, and that your joy might be full.*

*[12] This is my commandment, That ye love one another, as I have loved you.*

*[13] Greater love hath no man than this, that a man lay down his life for his friends.*

*[14] Ye are my friends, if ye do whatsoever I command you.*

*[15] Henceforth I call you not servants; for the servant knoweth not what his lord doeth: but I have called you friends; for all things that I have heard of my Father I have made known unto you.*

*[16] Ye have not chosen me, but I have chosen you, and ordained you, that ye should go and bring forth fruit, and that your fruit should remain: that whatsoever ye shall ask of the Father in my name, he may give it you.*

*[17] These things I command you, that ye love one another.*

*<sup>18</sup> If the world hate you, ye know that it hated me before it hated you.*

*<sup>19</sup> If ye were of the world, the world would love his own: but because ye are not of the world, but I have chosen you out of the world, therefore the world hateth you.*

*<sup>20</sup> Remember the word that I said unto you, The servant is not greater than his lord. If they have persecuted me, they will also persecute you; if they have kept my saying, they will keep yours also.*

*<sup>21</sup> But all these things will they do unto you for my name's sake, because they know not him that sent me.*

*<sup>22</sup> If I had not come and spoken unto them, they had not had sin: but now they have no cloak for their sin.*

*<sup>23</sup> He that hateth me hateth my Father also.*

*<sup>24</sup> If I had not done among them the works which none other man did, they had not had sin: but now have they both seen and hated both me and my Father.*

*<sup>25</sup> But this cometh to pass, that the word might be fulfilled that is written in their law, They hated me without a cause.*

*<sup>26</sup> But when the Comforter is come, whom I will send unto you from the Father, even the Spirit of truth, which proceedeth from the Father, he shall testify of me:*

*<sup>27</sup> And ye also shall bear witness, because ye have been with me from the beginning.*

**Day Forty   Sunday**          **John 13:1-17**(KJV)

**13** *Now before the feast of the passover, when Jesus knew that his hour was come that he should depart out of this world unto the Father, having loved his own which were in the world, he loved them unto the end.***²** *And supper being ended, the devil having now put into the heart of Judas Iscariot, Simon's son, to betray him;***³** *Jesus knowing that the Father had given all things into his hands, and that he was come from God, and went to God;***⁴** *He riseth from supper, and laid aside his garments; and took a towel, and girded himself.*

**⁵** *After that he poureth water into a bason, and began to wash the disciples' feet, and to wipe them with the towel wherewith he was girded.***⁶** *Then cometh he to Simon Peter: and Peter saith unto him, Lord, dost thou wash my feet?***⁷** *Jesus answered and said unto him, What I do thou knowest not now; but thou shalt know hereafter.***⁸** *Peter saith unto him, Thou shalt never wash my feet. Jesus answered him, If I wash thee not, thou hast no part with me.***⁹** *Simon Peter saith unto him, Lord, not my feet only, but also my hands and my head.***¹⁰** *Jesus saith to him, He that is washed needeth not save to wash his feet, but is clean every whit: and ye are clean, but not all.***¹¹** *For he knew who should betray him; therefore said he, Ye are not all clean.*

**¹²** *So after he had washed their feet, and had taken his garments, and was set down again, he said unto them, Know ye what I have done to you?***¹³** *Ye call me Master and Lord: and ye say well; for so I am.***¹⁴** *If I then, your Lord and Master, have washed your feet; ye also ought to wash one another's feet.***¹⁵** *For I have given you an example, that ye should do as I have done to you.*

**¹⁶** *Verily, verily, I say unto you, The servant is not greater than his lord; neither he that is sent greater than he that sent him.***¹⁷** *If ye know these things, happy are ye if ye do them.*

### Philippians 2:4-6(KJV)

**⁴** *Look not every man on his own things, but every man also on the things of others.***⁵** *Let this mind be in you, which was also in Christ Jesus:***⁶** *Who, being in the form of God, thought it not robbery to be equal with God:*

### Galatians 2:20(KJV)

**²⁰** *I am crucified with Christ: nevertheless I live; yet not I, but Christ liveth in me: and the life which I now live in the flesh I live by the faith of the Son of God, who loved me, and gave himself for me.*

**Daily Empowerment:**

When Jesus realized that He was embarking upon the last hours of His life as it was on earth, He did something amazing; rather than thinking about Himself, His heart was set on doing something for His disciples. He washed their feet, the dirtiest part of their bodies. What a wonderful example of servant hood. You have been fellowshipping with your prayer partner for 40 days. Take today and do something for them. Then determine five people that you want to be a blessing to.

I will bless my prayer partner today by:

1._____

2._____

3._____

Five things I am praying about today are:

1._____

2._____

3._____

4._____

5._____

Five People I Will Be a Blessing to Today are:

1._____

2._____

3._____

4._____

5._____

# TESTIMONIALS

*Use these pages to record at least 7 testimonials or events giving God the Glory in your life during this 40 Day period.*

_____
_____
_____
_____
_____
_____
_____
_____
_____
_____
_____
_____
_____
_____
_____
_____
_____
_____
_____
_____
_____
_____
_____
_____
_____
_____
_____
_____
_____
_____
_____
_____
_____
_____

**Continue Your Prayer Life with the Adullam Ministries, INC. Prayerline Every night at 7:00pm EST Dial (712)432-3900 Access Code 6949061**

Contact Adullam Ministries, INC at:

(678)329-7107

Send Correspondance and Donations to:

Adullam Ministries, INC
Power-Filled Prayer
3588 Highway 138 Suite 302
Stockbridge, Georgia 30281

Check out our Website and Blog at:

www.PowerFilledPrayer.org

Join our Facebook Group at:

https://www.facebook.com/PowerFilledPrayer